Alan Turing's
NUMBER GAMES
FOR KIDS

ARCTURUS

ARCTURUS

This edition published in 2022 by Arcturus Publishing Limited
26/27 Bickels Yard, 151–153 Bermondsey Street,
London SE1 3HA

Copyright © Arcturus Holdings Limited
The Turing Trust logo © The Turing Trust

All rights reserved. No part of this publication may be reproduced,
stored in a retrieval system, or transmitted, in any form or by any means,
electronic, mechanical, photocopying, recording, or otherwise, without
prior written permission in accordance with the provisions of the
Copyright Act 1956 (as amended). Any person or persons who do any
unauthorized act in relation to this publication may be liable to criminal
prosecution and civil claims for damages.

Author: Gemma Barder
Illustrator: Gareth Conway
Designer: Trudi Webb
Design Manager: Jessica Holliland
Managing Editor: Joe Harris

ISBN: 978-1-3988-2537-6
CH010456NT
Supplier 29, Date 0922, PI 0002156
Printed in China

What is STEM?

STEM is a world-wide initiative that aims to cultivate an interest in
Science, Technology, Engineering, and Mathematics, in an effort to
promote these disciplines to as wide a variety of students as possible.

ALL ABOUT ALAN

Alan Turing was born in London in 1912. He was a mathematical genius whose ideas helped develop modern computing.

During World War II, Alan played an important role at Bletchley Park in the UK. He helped design a machine called the "Bombe." The machine was used to decode messages from the German military.

Alan Turing's code-breaking skills helped the Allies shorten the war and saved many lives.

THE TURING TRUST

When you buy this book, you are supporting The Turing Trust. This is a charity, set up by Alan's family, in his memory.

The Turing Trust works with communities in Africa to give people access to computers.

Munching numbers

A greedy goat has eaten numbers from these calculations. Solve them in the order they appear, working from left to right, and from top to bottom in the grid.

5	+		−	3	=	9
−		+		+		
	×	6	+		=	22
×		×		−		
	×		+	7	=	27
=		=		=		
30		26		6		

Alan Turing's Challenge

Add up the answers to the horizontal and the vertical calculations. Which has the highest total?

Go fly a kite

These pairs of kites should be matching in every way, including their calculations. Spot the odd pair out.

$3 \times 3 =$ ___

$18 \div 6 =$ ___

$300 \div 30 =$ ___

$12 \div 4 =$ ___

$15 - 4 =$ ___

$2 \times 5 =$ ___

What a performance

Using the key, work out which of these performers was the most popular on ViewTube.

Key

= 3 points

= 5 points

= 10 points

= 15 points

Alan Turing's Challenge

Using the code a = 1, b = 2, c = 3, etc., add up all the numbers in the words Yellow, Green, and Blue. Which creates the highest number?

Beach treat

Shade multiples of 7 pink, multiples of 8 green, and
multiples of 11 orange to reveal a cool treat.

100	10	2	13	17	43	23	5	6	17	9	13
23	13	5	10	7	28	40	8	80	10	3	10
100	17	9	63	14	70	21	96	64	32	13	5
9	3	21	14	49	7	35	28	16	48	17	9
2	17	42	28	84	14	21	70	24	72	100	5
10	6	23	33	121	66	132	22	11	6	9	3
17	43	9	22	55	11	44	99	110	43	23	13
3	10	13	15	110	66	121	132	13	2	6	17
5	9	2	10	6	132	33	6	23	100	23	5
43	6	17	23	5	44	22	2	13	43	9	3

Pizza cutter

Welcome to the 360 Degrees Pizza restaurant, where the angles inside each pizza always add up to 360°! Can you work out the missing angles in each pizza?

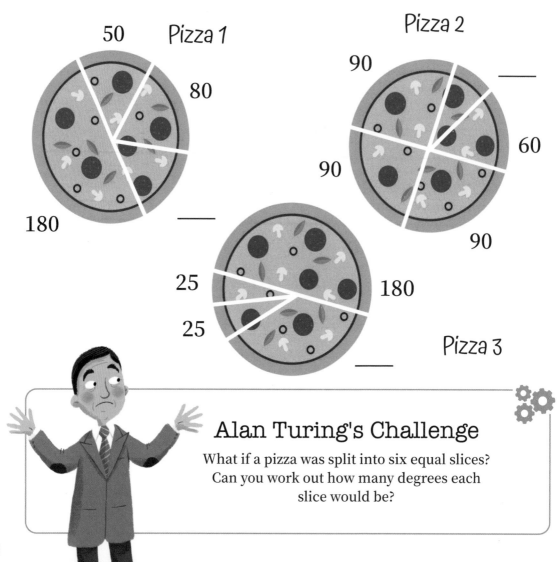

Pizza 1
50
80
180
___

Pizza 2
90
___
60
90
90

Pizza 3
25
25
180
___

Alan Turing's Challenge

What if a pizza was split into six equal slices? Can you work out how many degrees each slice would be?

Searching sandcastle

7	3	9	0	2	1	2	0	1	9
4	5	8	4	9	3	9	9	5	0
9	3	2	1	7	7	8	2	2	3
0	9	0	8	2	0	8	2	2	1
8	7	9	5	7	3	2	0	6	1
9	8	0	6	1	4	4	7	8	0
5	1	6	7	1	1	3	2	2	1
6	5	1	1	6	0	4	4	0	5

Find all these numbers in the grid. Numbers can appear across or down, not backward or diagonally.

23	45	84

321	405	567	978
2120	4478	8956	9727
11604	88243	90311	

Wilf the wizard

Answer all of Wilf's mystical questions by using the graph. The graph shows how many spells he cast for people in just one week!

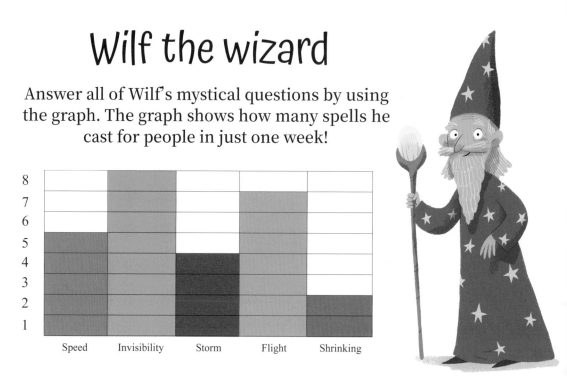

1 Which spell is twice as popular as the storm spell?

2 Which spell is half as popular as the storm spell?

3 How many spells did Wilf cast in total?

4 How many more people wanted to fly than to be speedy?

Alan Turing's Challenge

It takes Wilf 5 minutes to cast each spell. How many minutes did he spend casting spells this week?

Birthday beasts

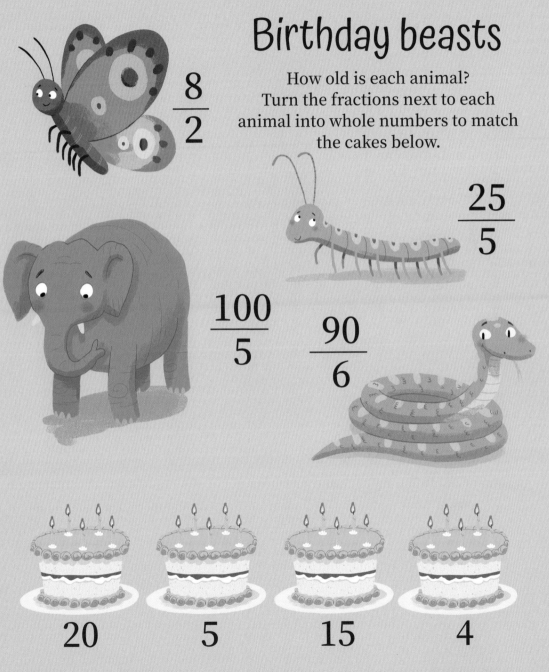

How old is each animal?
Turn the fractions next to each
animal into whole numbers to match
the cakes below.

$$\frac{8}{2}$$

$$\frac{25}{5}$$

$$\frac{100}{5}$$

$$\frac{90}{6}$$

20   5   15   4

Don't be shy

Each of these players has thrown three balls. Add up the numbers on the coconuts they hit to work out who has the highest total. That player is the winner!

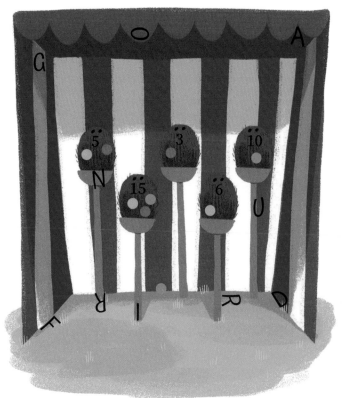

Green

Blue

Red

Alan Turing's Challenge

Look closely at the coconut shy. Can you see some letters hiding in the picture? Find them all and unscramble them to discover the place where a coconut shy might be found.

Rome at home

Work out what these Roman numerals mean, then draw
lines to match each number to the correct door.

Help your shelf

Dot is helping out at the library, but she can't work out the librarian's system. Can you help to put the books back on the correct shelves?

The shelf for the dictionary is the number of days in 6 weeks.

The shelf for the science book is the number of seconds in two minutes.

The shelf for the music book is the number of years in a century.

The shelf for the story book is the number of months in two years.

Alan Turing's Challenge

I've found one more book to go on the shelf! It has the Roman numeral XXV, which shelf should it go on?

Fishy goings on

Can you work out the correct order for these puzzle pieces? Write their numbers in the blank grid below. Pieces 2, 4, 7, 8, 9, 15, 16, and 17 are already in the correct positions.

Time trial

Work out which cyclist was the fastest around the track. The results of their time trials have been noted, below.

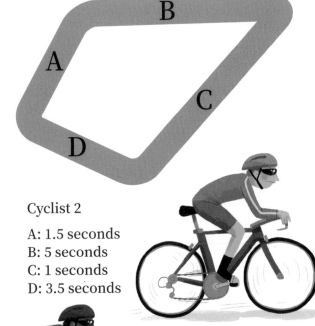

Cyclist 1

A: 4 seconds
B: 5 seconds
C: 1 seconds
D: 4 seconds

Cyclist 2

A: 1.5 seconds
B: 5 seconds
C: 1 seconds
D: 3.5 seconds

Cyclist 3

A: 2.5 seconds
B: 5 seconds
C: 1.5 seconds
D: 4 seconds

Alan Turing's Challenge

Which cyclist ended up with a time that was NOT a prime number? (Remember, a prime number can only be divided by itself and 1.)

Cupcake conclusion

Esmae is very particular about her cupcakes. Using her descriptions, can you figure out which one she wants?

 16

 14

 13

 18

 20

 10

My cupcake is an even number.

My cupcake is not a multiple of 6.

My cupcake is lower than 15.

My cupcake is in the 5 times table.

Treetop puzzling

Place a number from 1 to 9 into each empty square, so that the numbers in each row add up to the small number on the left, and numbers in the columns add up to the small number above.

Right on track

Which of these trains can carry the most passengers?

Train 1

Train 2

This train can carry 17 passengers in each carriage.

Train 3

This train carries 10 passengers in each of the red carts.

This train carries 11 passengers each in the first and last carriage, and 8 passengers in the middle carriage.

Train 4

This train carries 3 passengers for each blue window.

Alan Turing's Challenge

How many passengers could these trains carry all together?

Show time

Complete the calculation on each movie ticket to see which screen it is for.

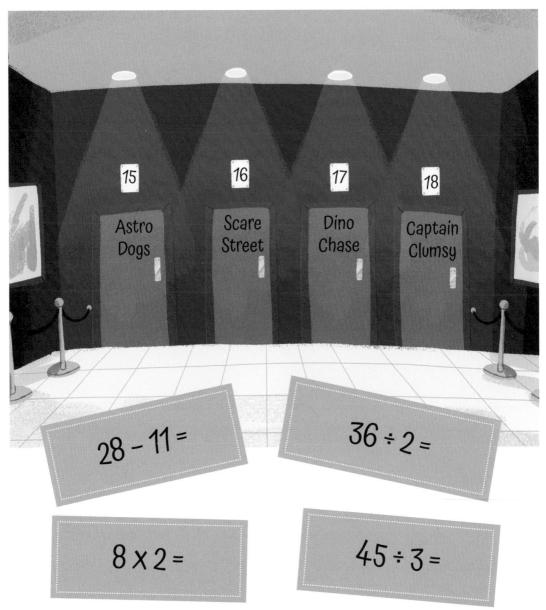

15 Astro Dogs

16 Scare Street

17 Dino Chase

18 Captain Clumsy

28 – 11 =

36 ÷ 2 =

8 x 2 =

45 ÷ 3 =

Missing parts

These robots are each missing a part. Work out which one they need from the group beside them. The correct piece will be the next number in the sequence.

3, 6, 9, 12, 15

12   14   18

1, 2, 4, 8

19   5   16

2, 3, 5, 7

5   11   4

10, 8, 6, 4

2   3   3   7

Penguin hop

Which three steps did each penguin take over the ice from the start to the bottom to reach their number? Each penguin starts with 1.

Start

+ 4

x 6

x 4

- 3

x 10

x 8

20

8

16

A tasty reward

5	24	67	52	16	12	60	24	30	7	50	12
47	13	82	7	79	20	5	95	10	79	16	32
10	52	20	30	93	43	98	32	20	52	93	6
60	16	32	89	24	52	54	27	67	12	43	95
26	36	43	6	47	81	36	63	45	67	47	10
12	54	81	26	9	72	90	99	81	18	30	82
89	45	18	36	54	45	18	54	99	72	36	43
5	63	72	60	27	63	90	36	72	45	26	52
50	9	16	7	52	81	45	63	9	60	24	50
24	79	93	20	32	24	27	54	95	5	20	89
95	82	30	10	60	6	47	93	79	82	67	79
7	95	47	52	93	50	12	79	7	32	16	6

After braving the ice, the penguins are looking for their lunch. Shade in all the numbers that are multiples of 9 to reveal their meal.

Alan Turing's Challenge

Take a piece of squared paper and see if you can create your own times-table challenge for a friend.

Dance off

The judges have very different opinions when it comes to scoring the dancing competition. Use their scores to answer the questions.

1 Which team had the lowest score?

2 Which team had the highest score?

3 Which team had the biggest difference between their highest and lowest score?

Ballroom Boyz

4 6 7 8

Team Tango

7 8 7 8

Hip Hop Hooray

5 7 7 10

Samba Stars

8 9 9 10

Alan Turing's Challenge

What was the average score for the dancing couples?
(Hint: Add the scores then divide by four.)

Furniture fit

Here's a view of a room, seen from above. Look at the measurements and then write in the missing sizes for the couch and armchair.

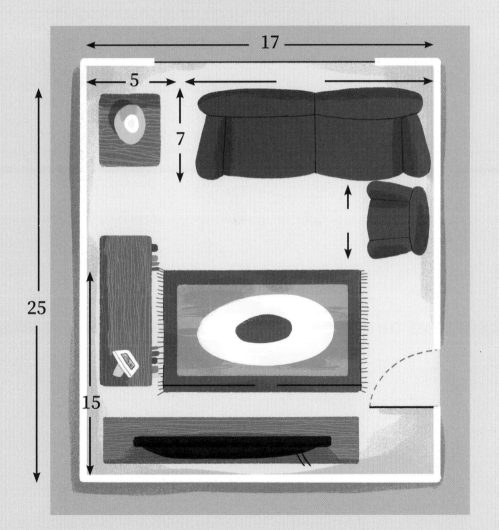

Strike up the band

Each instrument has a number to show how loud it is. Look at the totals for each row and column. If the violin is 5 and the guitar is 14, what number are the other instruments?

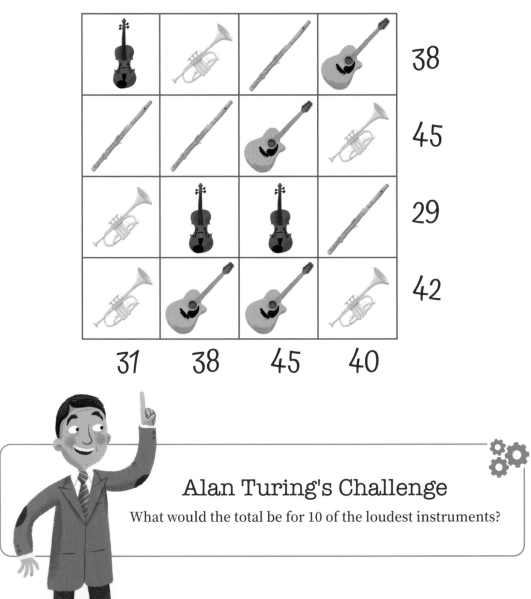

Alan Turing's Challenge

What would the total be for 10 of the loudest instruments?

Castle crumble

This castle needs a bit of rebuilding. Finish off the turrets by working out the missing numbers.

Turret 1:

7	×	3	=	
+				–
				19
=				=
13	–		=	2

Turret 2:

12	–	6	=	
+				×
				3
=				=
15	+		=	

Turret 3:

4	×		=	20
+				+
=				=
12	×	2	=	

A nice slice

Draw lines through each
cake to cut equal slices
for each party guest.

Party
one has
8 people

Party
two has
6 people

Party
three has
16 people

Alan Turing's Challenge

A full circle has 360 degrees. If 6 people have an equal slice
from the cake, how many degrees does each slice have?

Playful pups

Dog 1

There are two balls for each pup to play with. The ball numbers add up to the numbers beside each pup. Which balls belong to each pup?

13

7

5

Dog 2

17

12

Dog 3

14

8

2

10

X marks the spot

Captain Patch has buried his treasure somewhere on one of the islands. Use the coordinates to find the spot to dig and mark it with a cross.

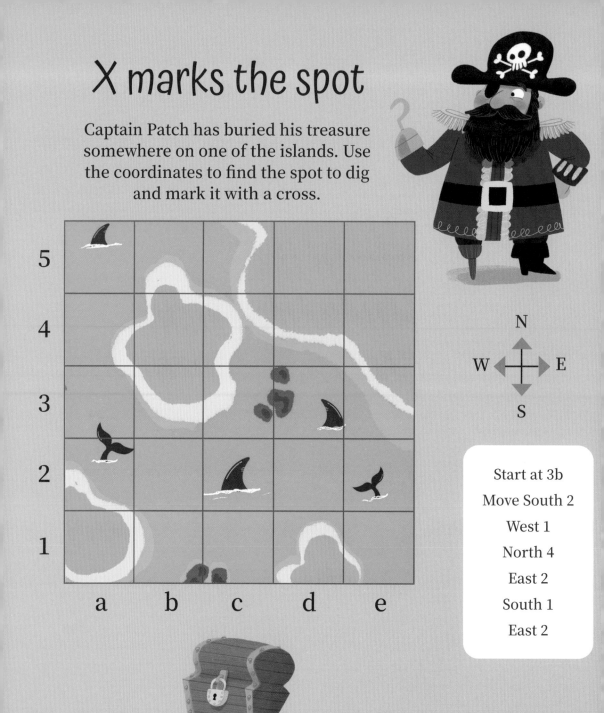

Start at 3b
Move South 2
West 1
North 4
East 2
South 1
East 2

Backstroke

Did you know that seahorses can swim backward? They also do their calculations backward! Work out the missing number in each equation by looking at the answer first.

$$24 = \underline{} \times 12$$

$$17 = \underline{} - 10$$

$$27 = 3 \times \underline{}$$

$$12 = 36 \div \underline{}$$

Alan Turing's Challenge

Use the code a = 1, b = 2, c = 3, etc. to work out the name of a bird that can fly backward.

8 21 13 13 9 14 7 2 9 18 4

Flower power

Fill in each row, column with numbers 1-6, but there's a floral twist! Two of the numbers have been replaced by flowers.

1	✿	3	4		✿
	✿		✿	1	
✿		✿		4	1
5	1	4		✿	✿
✿	4		✿	3	5
3		✿	1	✿	4

Key

✿ = 2

✿ = 6

32

Gridlock

Help the scientist place all the numbers on her board.

20	971
49	8541
190	9031
292	9329
681	722329
696	6592528
948	6917048

Alan Turing's Challenge

Which two of the answers adds up to 988?

Sleeping lions

The zookeeper keeps a careful eye on how long his lazy lions sleep. Can you work out which one slept the longest?

1

2

3

4

Lion 1 slept from 2pm to 5pm ate dinner then fell back to sleep from 9pm to 8am the next day.

Lion 2 slept from 12pm to 1pm, had lunch, then played until 6pm. She then fell asleep and didn't wake until 7am the next day.

Lion 3 slept from 12pm to 4pm, from 7pm to 3am the next day, and from 4am to 8am.

Lion 4 slept from 3pm to 5pm, then 9pm to 7am the next day.

Pack picker

Tilda has been given a number to collect her backpack from the cloakroom. Can you work out which bag is Tilda's from her number descriptions?

Tilda's backpack is lower than 30.

It is not an even number.

It is higher than 24.

Alan Turing's Challenge

My backpack is in the pile, too! It is the only number in the 7 times table.

Slippery numbers

Complete each calculation along the slide before moving on to the next. What number do you come up with at the end of each slide?

Slide 1: 50 ÷ 2 + 13 ÷ 5 − 2 − 10 × 2 + 6

Slide 2: 6 × 4 + 10 − 2 + 4 ÷ 2 − 11 + 2 − 5

Slide 3: 14 × 10 ÷ 2 + 3 ÷ 5 × 2 + 2 − 15 − 5

Slide 4: 100 − 30 × 2 − 45 + 4 + 1 ÷ 4

Alan Turing's Challenge

What figure do you get if you add up all four of the slides' results?

Start

4	10	42	63	75	95	21	42
8	12	18	50	21	13	35	63
63	16	22	13	38	77	21	14
42	20	24	28	30	89	25	50
62	63	75	32	38	21	95	63
10	44	40	36	42	43	63	13
50	48	46	42	68	72	76	70
63	52	56	60	64	96	80	84

Finish

Letters line up

Draw a continuous line through
the letters to deliver them to the
postal worker. Start at 4, then
add 4 for each letter. Draw your
lines going left, right, up and
down, but not diagonally.

A

B

C

Price list:

— 5 gold coins

🧁 2 gold coins

🍾 6 gold coins

🍄 3 gold coins—buy two toadstools and get one free!

Magical shopping list

Can you help the storekeeper to work out how much each fairy has spent in his store?

Alan Turing's Challenge

How old is the shopkeeper fairy? He is the amount of gold coins it costs to buy 5 wands, times the amount of gold coins it costs to buy 2 cupcakes.

Trick or treat?

Three children are going to share their Halloween treats equally between them. Take a look at the amounts for each candy. How many will each child get?

The children collected:

33 chocolates

18 lollipops

39 gummies

gummies

chocolates

lollipops

Soccer subs

Each of these soccer teams has one substitute. The three players in the team have numbers on their shirts that add up to their team name. The substitute wears the number left over. Which two players are subs?

Twenty-Five United

Thirty-Three Rovers

Ticket to ride

Each plane ticket contains a clue that will match it to its plane. Can you work out which plane matches each ticket?

Prime Express

Ticket one
47 29
43 31 41 37

Ticket two
49 56
35 7 21 42

Ticket three 9
5 81 77 23
13

Seventh Heaven

Oddball Air

Alan Turing's Challenge

The numbers on each ticket also add up to the number of passengers on each plane. Which plane carries the most?

Giuseppe's pizzeria

Giuseppe's pizzas are so popular, he's had a huge rush of orders! Work out how many of each pizza topping he is going to need.

For each topping named below, Giuseppe uses: 3 mushrooms, 1 pepper, 2 tomatoes, 5 olives, and 6 slices of pepperoni. So "olive" means 5 olives, and so on.

1 x mushroom, olive, and pepper pizza

2 x olive, pepperoni, and tomato pizzas

1 x mushroom and olive pizza

2 x pepperoni and pepper pizzas

1 x "The works" (that's all the toppings on one pizza!)

Ingredients list:

	Mushrooms
	Tomatoes
	Peppers
	Olives
	Pepperoni

Alan Turing's Challenge

Find my pick of the toppings by cracking this code.
a = 2, b = 4, c = 6, d = 8, and so on.
26, 42, 38, 16, 36, 30, 30, 26, 38

Pick a potion

Which number comes next in each
sequence of magic potions?

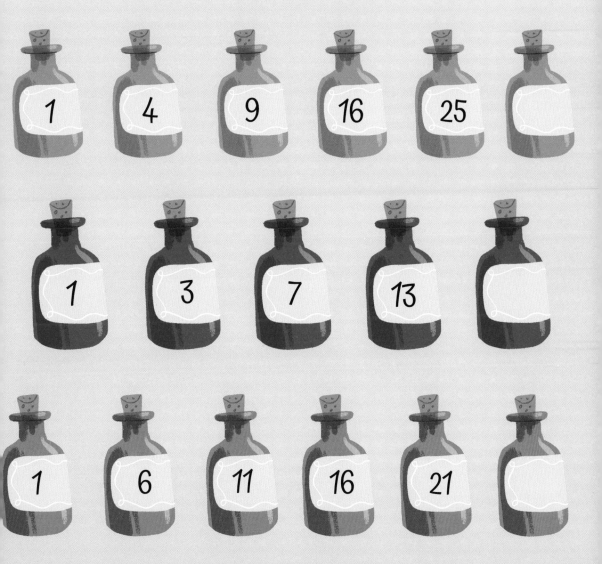

1   4   9   16   25

1   3   7   13

1   6   11   16   21

An evenly odd journey

Make your way through the jungle using the following code: odd, even, odd, even. You can move up, down, left, and right, but not diagonally.

Start

13	23	40	89	16	57
24	6	22	17	80	90
77	36	57	97	9	77
31	22	81	10	12	4
26	30	23	33	43	52
7	11	9	4	61	5

Finish

Fruit fans

These monkeys are about to share their stash of fruit equally. Work out what each monkey gets.

Alan Turing's Challenge

Now work out how much the monkeys would get if there were just two of them.

Coded cooking

Shade every number that is a multiple of 8 in brown and every multiple of 11 in red to reveal a tasty treat.

3	54	5	42	15	7	14	3	90	18	2	25
12	18	36	37	27	18	42	81	30	10	7	27
25	6	90	42	32	8	25	18	6	54	30	54
10	2	30	11	77	64	72	41	15	18	16	5
81	15	40	55	66	33	40	48	2	42	25	36
7	17	8	64	33	110	44	80	16	36	10	3
27	54	42	80	32	22	77	99	64	80	81	90
14	7	3	18	48	72	11	66	44	32	64	12
2	25	38	27	81	16	64	99	33	22	16	2
5	12	36	7	54	27	80	32	11	44	18	42
42	18	10	15	39	25	6	2	54	14	43	10
6	90	2	14	3	42	18	12	81	5	15	7

All that glitters ...

These jewels have been put into groups, but there is a fake in each set! Spot the number that doesn't belong in each group to find the fake.

Set 1

12 3 18 9 17

Set 2

9 3 7 1 4

Set 3

14 21 7 84 23

Alan Turing's Challenge

Now you know the fake jewels, work out the total of their numbers.

Bee helpful!

Help the bee get back to its hive. She can only fly between hexagons containing numbers from either the 2 or 5 times tables, or both.

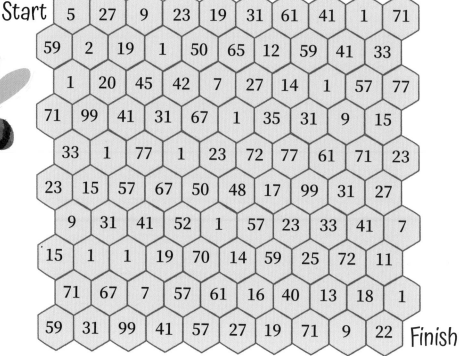

Start

| 5 | 27 | 9 | 23 | 19 | 31 | 61 | 41 | 1 | 71 |

| 59 | 2 | 19 | 1 | 50 | 65 | 12 | 59 | 41 | 33 |

| 1 | 20 | 45 | 42 | 7 | 27 | 14 | 1 | 57 | 77 |

| 71 | 99 | 41 | 31 | 67 | 1 | 35 | 31 | 9 | 15 |

| 33 | 1 | 77 | 1 | 23 | 72 | 77 | 61 | 71 | 23 |

| 23 | 15 | 57 | 67 | 50 | 48 | 17 | 99 | 31 | 27 |

| 9 | 31 | 41 | 52 | 1 | 57 | 23 | 33 | 41 | 7 |

| 15 | 1 | 1 | 19 | 70 | 14 | 59 | 25 | 72 | 11 |

| 71 | 67 | 7 | 57 | 61 | 16 | 40 | 13 | 18 | 1 |

| 59 | 31 | 99 | 41 | 57 | 27 | 19 | 71 | 9 | 22 |

Finish

Alan Turing's Challenge

Quick! Estimate the number of hexagons on the page without counting them. How close are you to the correct answer?

Beach life

The lifeguard uses a graph to estimate the number of swimmers at the beach each day. Can you answer all his questions?

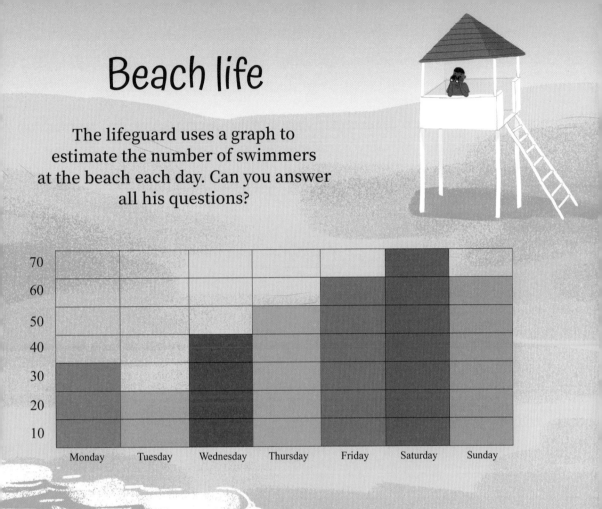

1 What was the least popular day at the beach?

2 How many days had 50 visitors or more?

3 How many more people visited on Sunday compared to Monday?

4 How many people in total visited at the weekend?

Stop, thief!

Help catch the jewel thieves! Solve the riddles to work out which door they are hiding behind.

RIDDLES

1. Mr. Jones has 5 sons, each of his sons has a sister. How many children does Mr. Jones have?

2. There are 6 cupcakes in a basket. If you take out 2, how many do you have?

3. The grandad was twice as old as his son. The grandson was a quarter the age of the son. If the grandson is 8, how old is the grandad?

6 2 64

10 4 32

6 4 64

10 2 80

Hop to it

Below which tree will each bunny come out?
Use your number skills to work it out!

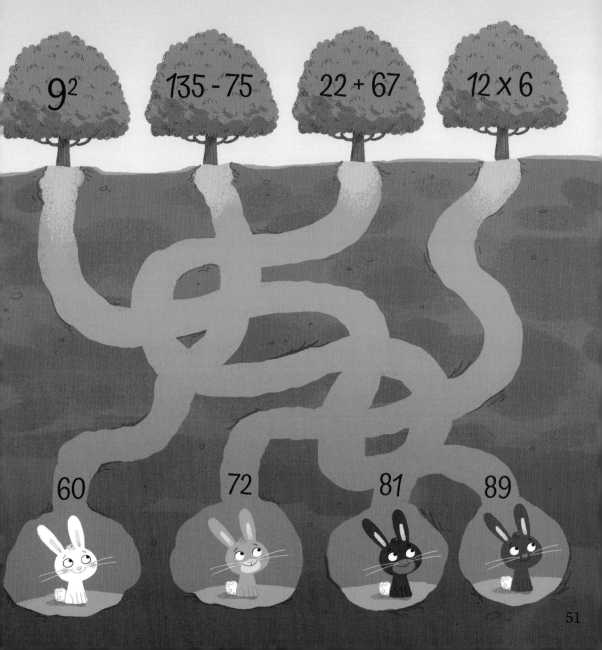

9^2

$135 - 75$

$22 + 67$

12×6

60

72

81

89

Puppy love

Help the puppy get back to her owner. Lead her through the park by only stepping on numbers in the 6 times table. You can move across, up, and down, but not diagonally.

Start

24	14	1	77	11	89	9	46	88	1
36	9	12	18	30	11	34	56	56	33
48	66	6	46	60	43	89	11	14	1
56	55	46	1	36	46	34	3	43	44
89	33	18	42	24	9	9	1	55	22
9	88	12	1	77	11	55	88	9	46
1	43	12	43	42	48	54	3	1	89
43	22	66	30	18	99	6	77	3	22
14	34	46	1	55	33	48	42	22	77
89	1	88	77	45	14	88	12	30	60

Finish

Not-so smart phones

What single-digit number are each of these message chains describing?

Message 1

I think the number is lower than 5.

I agree. It's also equal and prime.

The number is...

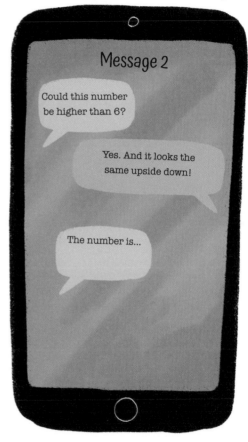

Message 2

Could this number be higher than 6?

Yes. And it looks the same upside down!

The number is...

Alan Turing's Challenge

In World War II, the quickest way to send messages was by telegram. What number is this telegram talking about?

Missing number is higher than 4 • Warning! It is lower than 10 • It is a number that is the square of another number

Alien adventure

Help Squib return to his home planet. Only a path following the 9 times table will take him to the right spaceship. You can move across, up, and down, but not diagonally.

Start

24	14	1	77	18	89	7	46	88	1
35	19	12	17	72	111	34	56	56	33
48	66	108	90	45	43	89	11	114	1
56	55	27	1	36	46	34	3	43	44
89	33	99	36	24	8	71	1	55	22
19	88	12	9	77	11	55	88	8	46
1	63	54	81	42	48	52	3	1	89
43	117	66	30	16	96	6	77	3	22
14	18	180	90	72	33	108	45	99	77
89	1	88	77	63	54	27	12	27	9

A new term

Miss Holmes gives each of the five children in her class the same amount of school supplies. How many of each item does each child get?

Alan Turing's Challenge

Uh-oh! We missed out Miss Holmes. If she takes one book, how many books will each child get and how many are left over?

Time trial

Which route should the delivery driver take to deliver all her parcels in the fastest time? The time it takes to go down each road is marked.

Route 1

Route 2

5 mins

3 mins

12 mins

8 mins

6 mins

2 mins

1 min

4 mins

4 mins

8 mins

1 min

2 mins

2 mins

End

Alan Turing's Challenge

What time does the postal worker finish Route One if she starts at 11.45am?

Climb to the top

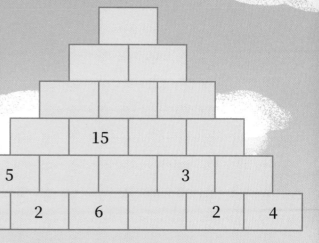

Help the climbers reach the top of the mountain by filling in each blank block. The number on each block is the sum of the numbers on the two blocks below it.

Nutty for nuts

This squirrel has hidden his acorns for winter, and now he can't remember where to find them! Follow the coordinates in the table below to locate his supplies and mark the square with a cross.

| 3 → | 4 ↓ | 2 ← | 3 ↓ | 4 → | 1 ↑ | 3 → | 4 ↑ | 2 ← | 3 ↓ | 2 ← | 3 ↑ |

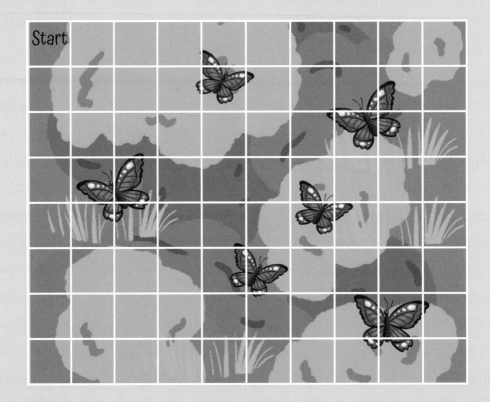

Start

58

Tricky timetable

It's Daisy's first day at school.
Help her work out how long
each lesson is.

	Start	Finish	How long?
English	9.00 am	9.45 am	
Mathematics	9.55 am	10.35 am	
Science	10.45 am	12.15 pm	
Art	1.30 pm	2.20 pm	
Sport	2.35 pm	3.30 pm	

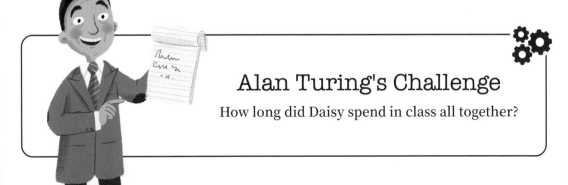

Alan Turing's Challenge

How long did Daisy spend in class all together?

Swim session

The London sponsored swim has raised lots of money for charity. Can you work out how much each team raised?

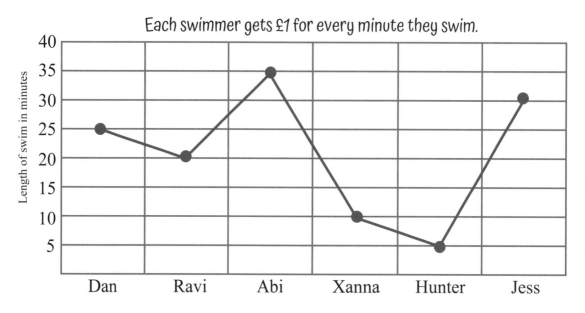

Each swimmer gets £1 for every minute they swim.

Length of swim in minutes

Dan — Ravi — Abi — Xanna — Hunter — Jess

Team one: Abi and Xanna
Team two: Dan and Jess
Team three: Ravi and Hunter

Alan Turing's Challenge

How much was raised in total?

Crowning glory

This fairy loves collecting flowers. What flower comes next in each sequence?

_____

_____

_____

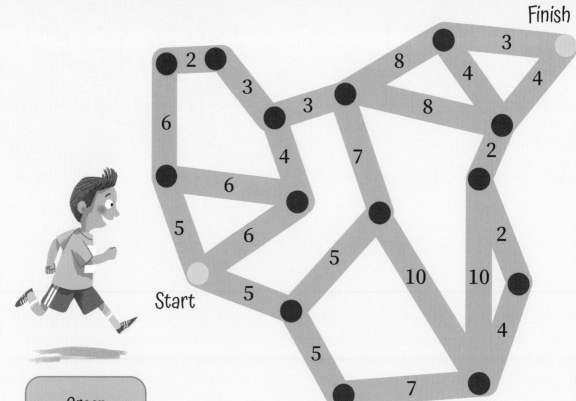

Finish

Start

Fun run

This map shows how many minutes it takes to run along each path. Can you work out which route each of these runners took?

Blast off

Finish this picture by joining the dots. Start at 4 and go up in multiples of 4.

48

50

44

38

34

40

52

54

32   36

56

28

62

18   24

60

What picture
do you get?

20
16

64

80   72

14   12   76

84

68

8   82   74

4 92 88

Alan Turing's Challenge

Using the backward alphabet code, Z = A, Y = B,
X = C, etc. can you work out the name of the first
mission that landed astronauts on the Moon?

Zklool vovevm

Weighing it up

To make this cake, put the four eggs and all the butter on one side of the scales. You will need two bags of flour and two bags of sugar to balance the scales. Which bags should you choose?

75   60

20   25

20   20   20   20

50   20

30   10

40   60

Race to the finish

Which racehorse won the race? Use the clues to figure out which number horse is the winner.

Clue 1: It is not a multiple of 10.
Clue 2: It appears in the 4 times table.
Clue 3: It is more than 5 x 7.

Alan Turing's Challenge

What fraction of the horses in the race have numbers that are multiples of 7?

Box clever

Take a look at these dice.
Only two have been made
using the pattern below.
Which two?

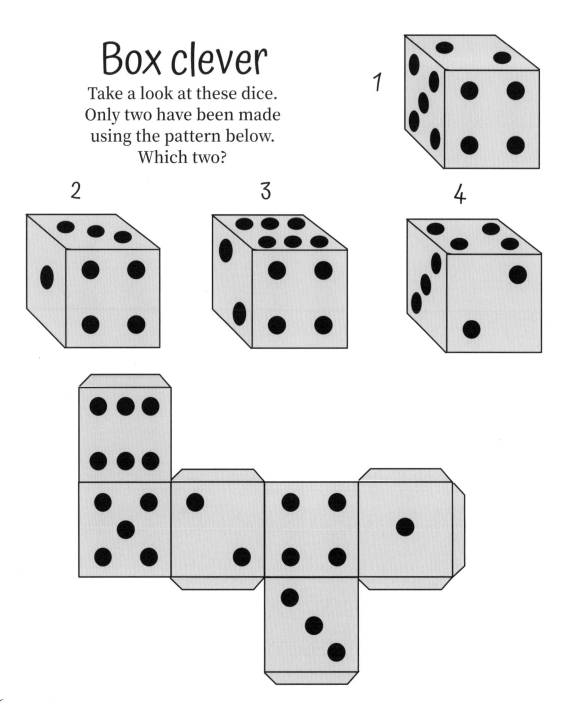

1

2

3

4

10	90	71	24		79	55	80	35
47	32	16	78	21	56	5	78	70
17	66	79	32	88	50	5	31	33
55	61	44	80	70	7	12	52	7
69	10	56	47	17	41	99	2	67
23	88	93	50	16	22	33	2	71
13	22	99	24	93	35	52	31	69
44	23	61	21	41	67	90	66	13

Find the pearl

Help the mermaid to find the shell that contains a shiny pearl! Cross out each shell with a matching number on the page. The leftover shell hides the pearl.

Jacket $30
T-shirt $25
Trainers $40
Jeans $20

2 pairs of trainers
1 pair of jeans

3 1 jacket
2 pairs of jeans

2 jackets
1 T-shirt
1 pair of jeans

1

2

5

1 pair of trainers
1 T-shirt

4

1 jacket
2 T-shirts
1 pair of trainers

Shopping trip

Look at the list of purchases from these
shopping trips. Which bag cost the most?

Alan Turing's Challenge

How much would you spend all together if you bought one
of each item: a jacket, T-shirt, pair of trainers, and jeans?

Scooter-doku

Scoot your way through this super puzzle!

	3	5	6		4	8	9	
8		2		7	3	5	6	
9	6	1	2	8			7	4
2		6	3		9	1	5	
4			8		7		2	6
	7	9	1	2	6			8
1		7	4	9				3
	9	4	7		8	2		
3	2		5		1	7		9

Fill in this grid making sure the numbers 1-9 only appear once in each row, column, and 3x3 mini-grid.

69

Butterfly fun

These butterflies are looking a bit dull. Work out what each of them should look like, using the percentages.

10% should be yellow.

20% should be blue.

20% should be green.

30% should be red.

5% should be black.

5% should be purple.

10% should be orange.

Alan Turing's Challenge

How many butterflies are neither red, nor blue, nor yellow?

Toy line up

Henry likes to order his toys by arranging them in repeated sequences. What comes next in each row?

Way out

Unlock these doors by using the symbols on each one to complete the calculations. Solve the calculations in the order in which they appear, working from left to right.

12 ☐ 4 ☐ 2 = 14

10 ☐ 12 ☐ 11 = 2

24 ☐ 15 ☐ 2 = 18

Leaf fall

Find all the numbers in the grid. Look left, right, up, down, backward, and diagonally.

7	6	5	4	3	2	1	2	1	2
6	0	2	3	1	8	6	4	5	6
4	4	3	6	5	9	2	1	5	7
5	9	7	6	7	5	0	4	8	9
8	9	9	7	3	6	4	2	0	0
1	0	9	8	4	7	6	8	4	0
7	2	0	3	7	9	8	8	0	1
7	5	1	3	2	1	7	7	6	6

1098
1776
4436
8766
26790
34601
123456

Alan Turing's Challenge

Add up the numbers on the corner leaves.
What do you get?

Number juggler

This performer has juggled all the letters to numbers in this message. Can you decode it?
The code is 1 = A, 2 = B, 3 = C, etc.

1 12 1 14

20 21 18 9 14 7

23 1 19   2 15 18 14

9 14   12 15 14 4 15 14

Alan Turing's Challenge

Look at these numbers in a mirror to work out the year I was born!

1912

Best of bugs

What creature can you see in the grid?
Shade all the numbers in the 5 times table red.

9	7	19	4	14	18	27	98	14	16	8	101	18
31	2	11	32	9	■	■	■	11	29	31	123	26
7	123	16	61	101	■	■	■	4	72	32	81	8
26	18	27	75	5	60	■	15	50	10	19	2	87
111	98	10	30	25	90	■	5	35	15	45	7	61
8	70	15	■	40	10	■	60	25	■	75	20	98
72	10	35	25	65	20	■	30	70	5	50	65	111
87	50	20	100	■	60	■	20	■	15	90	30	7
7	61	45	5	15	70	■	10	55	100	25	26	87
32	9	81	30	15	55	■	10	40	90	32	4	87
8	101	18	98	2	31	■	61	19	7	111	9	31

Hot dog hustle

Line up for hot dogs! Answer the questions below to see how many you could buy.

Plain hot dogs:
$2.50

Hot dog
with mustard
$3.00

Hot dog with
mustard & ketchup
$3.50

Fries $2

1 You have $10 and want to buy two hot dogs and two portions of fries. If you use all your money, which hot dogs could you get?

2 You have $5 and want two hot dogs. Which hot dogs could you get?

3 You have $14 and need to get four hot dogs and two portions of fries. Which hot dogs can you afford?

Alan Turing's Challenge

How much change would you have from $10 if you wanted one hot dog with mustard and ketchup, and one portion of fries?

Building the hive

Help the beekeeper keep track of the bees in the hive by filling in the missing numbers.

The top three rows have numbers equal to the two numbers below added together.

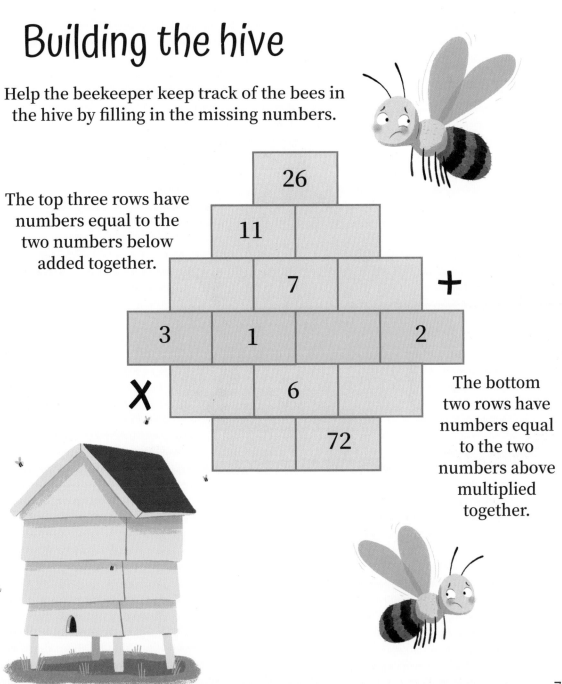

The bottom two rows have numbers equal to the two numbers above multiplied together.

26

11

7

3   1   2

+

×

6

72

Tricky tractor

Fill in the missing numbers to get the tractor moving.

The number in each shaded segment is the answer when the numbers in the white segments that touch it are added together.

Alan Turing's Challenge

After you have solved the puzzle, how many numbers on the wheels can you see that are exactly divisible by 5?

Slippery spots

Join only the dots that are square numbers to reveal the coolest bird on the planet. Start at 1 and go up.

Eggs-iting collection!

How many eggs have been collected? Make your way around the maze adding up the numbers on the correct route to find out!

Start

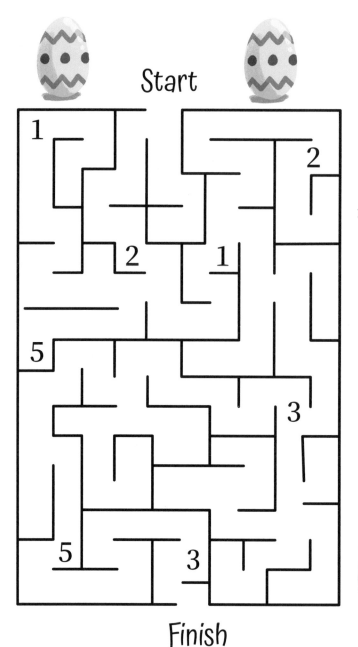

1

2

2

1

5

3

5

3

Finish

Clever cards

Work out which hand of cards will be the winner in each game with three players.

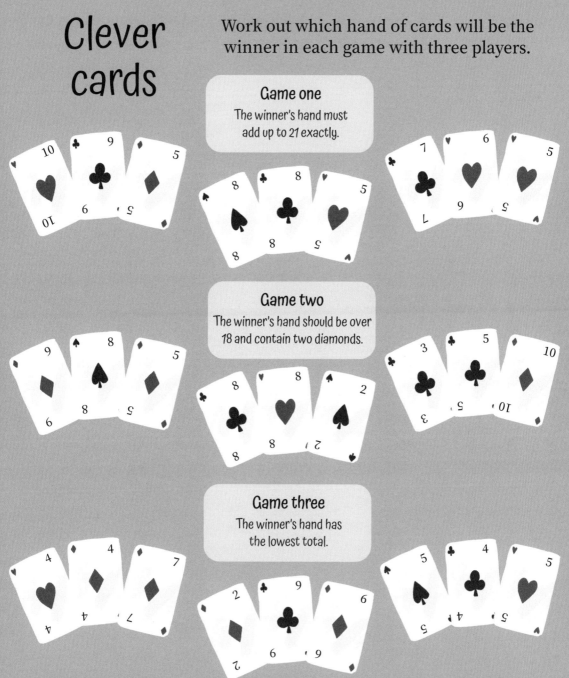

Game one
The winner's hand must add up to 21 exactly.

Game two
The winner's hand should be over 18 and contain two diamonds.

Game three
The winner's hand has the lowest total.

Speedy sale

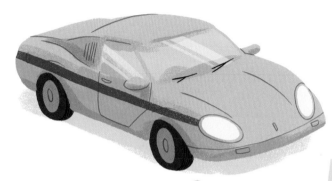

This remote-controlled car is being sold in four different stores. Which price is best?

Offer 1:
WAS $80
NOW half price

Offer 2:
WAS $60
NOW one third off

Offer 3:
WAS $100
NOW 65% off

Offer 4:
WAS $110,
NOW 50% off

Alan Turing's Challenge

Which is the worst deal?

Wizard's code

Find the magic number to cast the spell! Fill each row, column, and 2x2 mini-grid with the numbers 1-4. When the grid is complete, each of the corners will reveal the magic number. Read the number clockwise from the top left corner.

	2		
		1	
2			4
4	3		

Zoo time

It's feeding time. Zookeeper Jake starts at 10.30am. It takes 40 minutes to feed the giraffes, 45 minutes to feed the penguins, and 30 minutes to feed the zebras. After his own one-hour lunch break, Jake feeds the lions. That takes 25 minutes. What time does Jake finish feeding all the animals?

Puzzle
SOLUTIONS!

No peeking here until you've given each puzzle your best shot! If you get stuck, try rereading the instructions carefully.

Solutions

Page 4

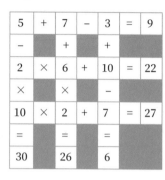

5	+	7	–	3	=	9
–		+		+		
2	×	6	+	10	=	22
×		×		–		
10	×	2	+	7	=	27
=		=		=		
30		26		6		

Alan Turing's Challenge
Horizontal: 9 + 22 + 27 = 58
Vertical: 30 + 26 + 6 = 62

Page 5

The pink kites are the odd ones out.

Pink:
3 × 3 = 9   15 – 4 = 11

Bird:
2 × 5 = 10   300 ÷ 30 = 10

Blue and yellow:
12 ÷ 4 = 3   18 ÷ 6 = 3

Page 6

Magician: 28 points

Guitarist: 31 points

Violinist: 30 points

The guitarist was the most popular.

Alan Turing's Challenge
Yellow = 92
Green = 49
Blue = 40

Page 7

100	10	2	13	17	43	23	5	6	17	9	13
23	13	5	10	7	28	40	8	80	10	3	10
100	17	9	63	14	70	21	96	64	32	13	5
9	3	21	14	49	7	35	28	16	48	17	9
2	17	42	28	84	14	21	70	24	72	100	5
10	6	23	33	121	66	132	22	11	6	9	3
17	43	9	22	55	11	44	99	110	43	23	13
3	10	13	15	110	66	121	132	13	2	6	17
5	9	2	10	6	132	33	6	23	100	23	5
43	6	17	23	5	44	22	2	13	43	9	3

Page 8

Pizza 1 = 50°, Pizza 2 = 30°

Pizza 3 = 130°

Alan Turing's Challenge
Six equal slices = 60°

Page 9

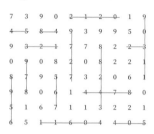

Page 10

1. Invisibility

2. Shrinking

3. 26

4. 2

Alan Turing's Challenge
130 minutes, or 2 hours and 10 minutes.

Page 11

Butterfly = 4

Elephant = 20

Snake = 15

Caterpillar = 5

Solutions

Page 12

25   23   26

Alan Turing's Challenge
FAIRGROUND

Page 13

VIII (8)

XI (11)

IV (4)

XIII (13)

VI (6)

Page 14

Dictionary: 42

Science book: 120

Music book: 100

Story book: 24

Alan Turing's Challenge
25

Page 15

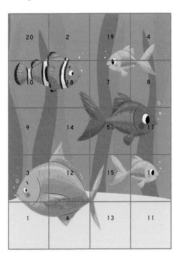

Page 16

Cyclist 1: 14 seconds

Cyclist 2: 11 seconds

Cyclist 3: 13 seconds

Alan Turing's Challenge
Cyclist 1

Page 17

10

Page 18

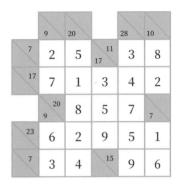

Page 19

Train 2 can carry most passengers.

Train 1: 51

Train 2: 30

Train 3: 30

Train 4: 42

Alan Turing's Challenge
153

Page 20

$28 - 11 = 17$

$36 \div 2 = 18$

$8 \times 2 = 16$

$45 \div 3 = 15$

Solutions

Page 21

Three times table:
3, 6, 9, 12, 15, (18)

Minus two:
10, 8, 6, 4, (2)

Double last number:
1, 2, 4, 8, (16)

Prime numbers:
2, 3, 5, 7, (11)

Page 22

$1 + 4 - 3 \times 10 = 20$

$1 + 4 - 3 \times 8 = 16$

$1 \times 4 - 3 \times 8 = 8$

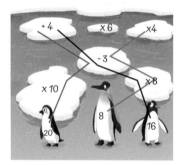

Page 23

5	24	67	52	16	12	60	24	30	7	50	12
47	13	82	7	79	20	5	95	10	79	16	32
10	52	20	30	93	43	98	32	20	52	93	6
60	16	32	89	24	52	54	27	67	12	43	95
26	36	43	6	47	81	36	63	45	67	47	10
12	54	81	26	9	72	90	99	81	18	30	82
89	45	18	36	54	45	18	54	99	72	36	43
5	63	72	60	27	63	90	36	72	45	26	52
50	9	16	7	52	81	45	63	9	60	24	50
24	79	93	20	32	24	27	54	95	5	20	89
95	82	30	10	60	6	47	93	79	82	67	79
7	95	47	52	93	50	12	79	7	32	16	6

Page 24

1: Ballroom Boys (25)

2: Samba Stars (36)

3: Hip Hop Hooray (10 - 5 = 5)

Alan Turing's Challenge
$25 + 29 + 36 = 120$, $120 \div 4 = 30$

Page 25

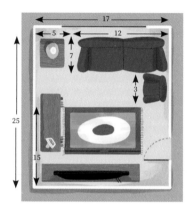

Page 26

Violin: 5

Trumpet: 7

Flute: 12

Guitar: 14

Alan Turing's Challenge
$10 \times 14 = 140$

Solutions

Page 27

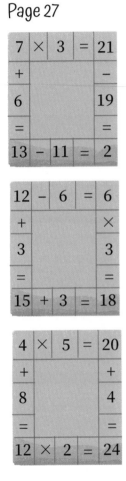

7	×	3	=	21
+				−
6				19
=				=
13	−	11	=	2

12	−	6	=	6
+				×
3				3
=				=
15	+	3	=	18

4	×	5	=	20
+				+
8				4
=				=
12	×	2	=	24

Page 28

Party 1

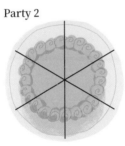

Party 2

Party 3

Alan Turing's Challenge

60 degrees

Page 29

Dog 1: 13 (8 + 5)

Dog 2: 17 (7 + 10)

Dog 3: 14 (12 + 2)

Page 30

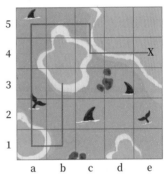

Page 31

$24 = 2 \times 12$

$17 = 27 - 10$

$27 = 3 \times 9$

$12 = 36 \div 3$

Alan Turing's Challenge

Hummingbird

Solutions

Page 32

Page 33

Alan Turing's Challenge
292 + 696 = 988

Page 34

Lion 1: 14 hours

Lion 2: 14 hours

Lion 3: 16 hours

Lion 4: 12 hours

Page 35

27

Alan Turing's Challenge
21

Page 36

1. $50 \div 2 \div 5 + 13 - 2 - 10 \times 2 + 6 = 18$

2. $6 \times 4 + 10 - 2 \div 2 + 4 - 5 + 2 - 11 = 6$

3. $14 \div 2 + 3 \times 10 \div 5 \times 2 - 15 + 2 - 5 = 22$

4. $100 - 30 \times 2 - 45 + 4 + 1 \div 4 = 25$

Alan Turing's Challenge
71

Page 37

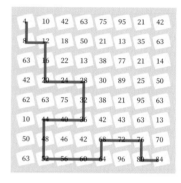

Page 38

A: 9 gold coins

B: 12 gold coins, as one toadstool is free

C: 16 gold coins

Alan Turing's Challenge
$25 \times 4 = 100$

Page 39

The children will each get 11 chocolates, 6 lollipops, and 13 gummies

Solutions

Page 40

Twenty-Five United: 4

Thirty-Three Rovers: 10

Page 41

Prime Express: Ticket 1 (all prime numbers) 29, 31, 37, 41, 43, 47

Seventh Heaven: Ticket 2 (all in the 7 times table) 7, 21, 35, 42, 49, 56

Oddball Air: Ticket 3 (all odd numbers) 5, 9, 13, 23, 77, 81

Alan Turing's Challenge

Prime Express takes the most passengers—228.

Page 42

9 Mushrooms

6 Tomatoes

4 Peppers

25 Olives

30 Pepperoni

Alan Turing's Challenge

Mushrooms

Page 43

1, 4, 9, 16, 25 (36 – they increase by adding ascending odd numbers)

1, 3, 7, 13, (21 – they increase by adding ascending even numbers)

1, 6, 11, 16, 21 (26 – they increase by adding 5s)

Page 44

15	23	40	89	16	57
24	6	22	17	80	90
77	36	57	97	9	77
31	22	81	10	12	4
26	30	23	33	43	52
7	11	9	4	61	5

Page 45

Each monkey gets:

2 bananas

3 oranges

1 apple

Alan Turing's Challenge

3 bananas

4½ oranges

1½ apples

Page 46

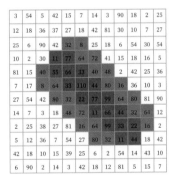

Solutions

Page 47

Set 1: 3, 9, 12, 17, 18
(17 is the odd one out because it is not a multiple of 3)

Set 2: 1, 3, 4, 7, 9
(4 is the odd one out because it is an even number)

Set 3: 7, 14, 21, 23, 84
(23 is the odd one out because it is not a multiple of 7)

Alan Turing's Challenge

17 + 4 + 23 = 44

Page 48

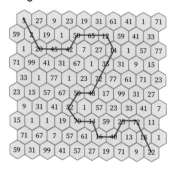

Alan Turing's Challenge

100

Page 49

1. Tuesday

2. 4

3. 30

4. 130

Page 50

Riddles
1. 6 (They share the one sister!)

2. 2 (The ones you took!)

3. 64

The red door.

Page 51

Page 52

24	14	1	77	11	89	9	46	88	1
36	9	12	18	30	11	34	56	56	33
48	66	6	46	60	43	89	11	14	1
56	55	46	1	36	46	34	3	43	44
89	33	18	42	24	9	9	1	55	22
9	88	12	1	77	11	55	88	9	46
1	43	12	43	42	48	54	3	1	89
43	22	66	30	18	99	6	77	3	22
14	34	46	1	55	33	48	42	22	77
89	1	88	77	45	14	88	12	30	60

Solutions

Page 53

Message 1: 2

Message 2: 8

Alan Turing's Challenge

9

Page 54

24	14	1	77	18	89	7	46	88	1
36	19	12	17	72	111	34	56	56	33
48	66	108	90	45	43	89	11	114	1
56	55	27	1	36	46	34	3	43	44
89	33	99	36	24	8	71	1	55	22
19	88	12	9	77	11	55	88	9	46
1	63	54	81	42	48	52	3	1	89
43	117	66	30	16	96	6	77	3	22
14	18	180	90	72	33	108	45	99	77
89	1	88	77	63	54	27	12	27	9

Page 55

2 pencils

1 eraser

5 books

1 ruler

Alan Turing's Challenge

4 books each with 4 left over.

Page 56

Route 1 takes 31 minutes.

Route 2 takes 27 minutes.

The driver should take Route 2.

Alan Turing's Challenge

12.16 p.m.

Page 57

Row 5: 97

Row 4: 53, 44

Row 3: 28, 25, 19

Row 2: 13, 15, 10, 9

Row 1: 5, 8, 7, 3, 6

Base: 3, 2, 6, 1, 2, 4

Page 58

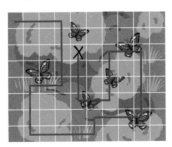

Page 59

	Start	Finish	How Long?
English	9.00 am	9.45 am	45 minutes
Mathematics	9.55 am	10.35 am	40 minutes
Science	10.45 am	12.15 pm	1 hr 30 mins
Art	1.30 pm	2.20 pm	50 minutes
Sport	2.35 pm	3.30 pm	55 minutes

Alan Turing's Challenge

4 hours, 40 minutes

Page 60

Team one: £45

Team two: £55

Team three: £25

Alan Turing's Challenge

£125

Page 61

Solutions

Page 62

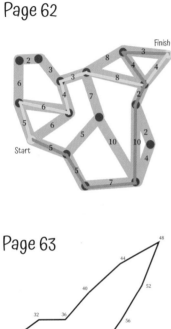

Page 63

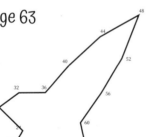

Alan Turing's Challenge
Apollo Eleven

Page 64

Eggs 4 × 20 = 80

Butter 40 + 60 = 100

Eggs + butter = 180

Flour: 75 + 25 = 100

Sugar 50 + 30 = 80

Flour + sugar = 180

Page 65

Horse 44

Alan Turing's Challenge
28 and 42 are multiples of 7, which is 2/5.

Page 66

Dice 2 and 3

Page 67

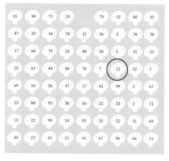

Page 68

Bag 4 is the most expensive.

Bag 1: $105

Bag 2: $100

Bag 3: $70

Bag 4: $120

Bag 5: $65

Alan Turing's Challenge
$115

Page 69

7	3	5	6	1	4	8	9	2
8	4	2	9	7	3	5	6	1
9	6	1	2	8	5	3	7	4
2	8	6	3	4	9	1	5	7
4	1	3	8	5	7	9	2	6
5	7	9	1	2	6	4	3	8
1	5	7	4	9	2	6	8	3
6	9	4	7	3	8	2	1	5
3	2	8	5	6	1	7	4	9

Solutions

Page 70

There should be:

2 yellow butterflies, 4 blue, 4 green, 6 red, 1 black, 1 purple, and 2 orange

Alan Turing's Challenge
8

Page 71

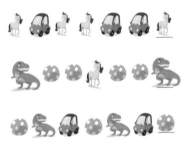

Page 72

Red door : 24 − 15 × 2 = 18

Blue door: 12 + 4 − 2 = 14

Purple door: 10 + 12 ÷ 11 = 2

Page 73

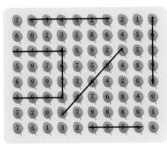

Alan Turing's Challenge
22

Page 74

Alan Turing was born in London

Alan Turing's Challenge
1912

Page 75

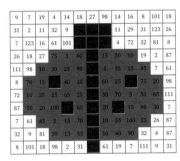

Page 76

1. 2 hot dogs with mustard.
2. 2 plain hot dogs.
3. 4 plain hot dogs.

Alan Turing's Challenge
$4.50

Page 77

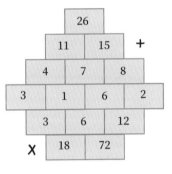

Page 78

Alan Turing's Challenge
6 (15, 15, 40, 45, 45 and 60)

Page 79

Page 80

14 eggs have been collected

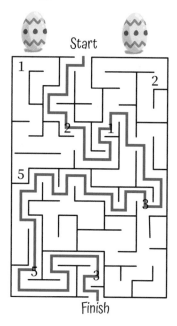

Page 81

Game one:

Game two:

Game three:

Page 82

Offer 3 is the best deal.

Offer 1: $40

Offer 2: $40

Offer 3: $35

Offer 4: $55

Alan Turing's Challenge

Offer 4 is the worst deal.

Page 83

1	2	4	3
3	4	1	2
2	1	3	4
4	3	2	1

The magic number is 1314.

Page 84

1.50 p.m.